TO:

-------------------------------------------------------------

Jesus said, "I tell you the truth, my Father
will give you whatever you ask in my name.
Until now you have not asked for anything
in my name. ASK AND YOU WILL RECEIVE,
and your joy will be complete." (John 16:23–24)


FROM:

-------------------------------------------------------------

*The Promise of Answered Prayer*
Copyright © 2003 by Zondervan
ISBN 0-310-98905-1

All Scripture quotations, unless otherwise noted, are taken from
the *Holy Bible: New International Version*, (North American
Edition)®. Copyright 1973, 1978, 1984, by International Bible
Society. Used by permission of Zondervan. All rights reserved.

The "NIV" and "New International Version" trademarks are
registered in the United States Patent and Trademark Office by
International Bible Society.

Requests for information should be addressed to:
Inspirio, The gift group of Zondervan
Grand Rapids, Michigan 49530
http://www.inspiriogifts.com

Compiler: Doris Rikkers
Editor: Janice Jacobson
Product Manager: Amy J. Wenger
Design: Lookout Design Group, Inc.

Printed in China
03 04 05/HK/ 4 3 2

# THE
# PROMISE OF
# ANSWERED
# PRAYER

## JIM CYMBALA

inspirio™

# CONTENTS

Jesus said, "If you believe,

you will receive whatever

you ask for in prayer."

— M A T T H E W   2 1 : 2 2

# THE POWER
## OF PERSONAL
### PRAYER

*Prayer is the source of the Christian life,*
*a Christian's lifeline.*

# GOD IS FAITHFUL

The Brooklyn Tabernacle—this woeful church that my father-in-law had coaxed me into pastoring—consisted of a shabby two-story building in the middle of a downtown block on Atlantic Avenue. The sanctuary could hold fewer than two hundred people—not that we required anywhere near that much capacity. The ceiling was low, the walls needed paint, the windows were dingy, and the bare wood floor hadn't been sealed in years. But there was no money for such improvements.

I shall never forget that first Sunday morning offering: $85. The church's monthly mortgage payment was $232, not to mention the utility bills or having anything left over for a pastoral salary.

When the first mortgage payment rolled around at the end of the month, the checking account showed something like $160 in hand. We were going to default right off the bat. I remember saying, "Lord, you have to help me. I don't know much—but I *do* know that we have to pay this mortgage."

When the mail came on Tuesday there was nothing but bills and fliers. Now I was trapped. I went upstairs, sat at my little desk, put my head down, and began to cry. "God," I sobbed, "what can I do? We can't even pay the mortgage." That night was the midweek service, and I knew there wouldn't be more than three or four people attending. The offering would probably be less than ten dollars. How was I going to get through this?

I called out to the Lord for a full hour or so. Eventually, I dried my tears—and a new thought came. *Wait a minute! Besides the mail slot in the front door, the church also has a post office box. I'll go across the street and see what's there. Surely God will answer my prayer!*

With renewed confidence I walked across the street, crossed the post office lobby, and twirled the knob on the little box. I peered inside. . . . Nothing. I trudged wearily back across the street to the little building.

As I unlocked the door, I was met with another surprise. There on the foyer floor was something that hadn't been there just three minutes earlier: a simple white envelope. With trembling hands I opened it to find...*two $50 bills.*

I began shouting all by myself in the empty church. "God, you came through! You came through!" We had $160 in the bank, and with this $100 we could make the mortgage payment. My soul let out a deep "Hallelujah!" What a lesson for a disheartened young pastor!

To this day I don't know where that money came from. I only know it was a sign to me that God was near—and faithful.

Every good and perfect gift is from above,
coming down from the Father of the heavenly lights,
who does not change like shifting shadows.

—JAMES 1:17

# ASK AND RECEIVE

God says to us, "Pray, because I have all kinds
of things for you; and when you ask, you will receive.
I have all this grace, and you live with scarcity. Come
unto me, all you who labor. Why are you so rushed?
Where are you running *now?* Everything you need,
I have."

If the times are indeed as bad as we say they are
. . . if the darkness in our world is growing heavier by
the moment . . . if we are facing spiritual battles right
in our own homes and churches . . . then we are
foolish not to turn to the One who supplies unlimited
grace and power. He is our only source. We are crazy
to ignore him.

"Ask and it will be given to you; seek and you will find; knock and the door will be opened to you. For everyone who asks receives; he who seeks finds; and to him who knocks, the door will be opened."

—MATTHEW 7:7-8

You do not have, because you do not ask God.

—JAMES 4:2

Be joyful always; pray continually; give thanks in all circumstances, for this is God's will for you in Christ Jesus.

—1 THESSALONIANS 5:16-18

# PRAY TOGETHER—
# STAY TOGETHER

Over the last 30 years, more books have been written about marriage than in all the preceding 2,000 years of church history. But ask any pastor in America if there aren't proportionally more troubled marriages today then in any other era. We have all the how-tos, but homes are still falling apart.

The couple that prays together stays together. I don't mean to be simplistic; there will be difficult moments in any union. But God's Word is true when it says, "Call upon me, and I will help you. Just give me a chance."

The same holds true for parenting. We may own stacks of good books on child rearing and spending "quality time" with our children. Yet we have more problems per 100 young people in the church today than at any previous time. This is not because we lack knowledge or how-to; it is because we have not cried out for the power and grace of God.

What if, in the last 25 years, we had invested only half the time and energy in writing, publishing, reading, and discussing books on the Christian family . . . and put the other half into praying for our marriages and our children? I am certain we would be in far better shape today.

*The greatest answer to prayer is more prayer.*

—SAMUEL CHADWICK

*Lord, give me patience in tribulation*

*and grace in everything to conform*

*my will to thine; that I may truly say:*

*"The things, good Lord, that I pray for,*

*give me thy grace to labour for."*

—ST. THOMAS MORE

# ACCORDING TO GOD'S WILL

I am well aware that we don't get everything
we ask for; we have to ask according to God's will.
But let us not use theological dodges to avoid the
fact that we often go without things God wants us
to have right now, today, because we fail to ask.
Too seldom do we get honest enough to admit,
"Lord, I can't handle this alone. I've just hit the
wall for the thirty-second time and *I need you.*"

> The words of the old hymn ring true:
> *Oh, what peace we often forfeit,*
> *Oh, what needless pain we bear,*
> *All because we do not carry*
> *Everything to God in prayer.*

God has chosen prayer as his channel of blessing.
He has spread a table for us with every kind of
wisdom, grace, and strength because he knows
exactly what we need. But the only way we can get
it is to pull up to the table and taste and see that
the Lord is good.

# PRECIOUS TREASURE

The book of Revelation says that when the twenty-four elders eventually fall at the feet of Jesus, each one will have a golden bowl—and do you know what's in the bowls? What is this incense that is so fragrant to Christ? "The prayers of the saints."

Just imagine . . . you and I kneel or stand or sit down to pray, really opening our hearts to God—and what we say is so precious to him that he keeps it like a treasure.

And when he had taken [the scroll],
the four living creatures and the twenty-four
elders fell down before the Lamb.
Each one had a harp and they were holding
golden bowls full of incense, which are
the prayers of the saints.

—REVELATION 5:8

# ASK FOR GREAT THINGS

*We always ask for less than we should*

*and don't even think God is willing to give*

*us what we ask for. We don't ask the right way.*

*We don't understand that what we pray about*

*is more important than we can comprehend.*

*We think small, but the Lord is great and powerful.*

*He expects us to ask for great things.*

*He wants to give them to us to demonstrate*

*his almighty power.*

—MARTIN LUTHER

# NEAR TO GOD

We have the opportunity right now to draw near to God in prayer, knowing that he will be faithful to draw near to us. Only the Lord can deliver us from busy, cluttered living that so easily drifts from the plan God has for our lives, from the spiritual fruit we can produce for his glory. What stops us at this moment from asking God to melt our hearts and soften our wills so we can be doers, not just hearers, of his Word?

*Prayer moves the hand of God,*
*a hand that is omnipotent.*

DEAR FATHER, FORGIVE US
FOR OFTEN IGNORING YOUR
PURPOSE FOR OUR LIVES.
PARDON US FROM THE SIN
OF SMALL AND SELFISH
LIVING, WITH LITTLE
THOUGHT OF THE PRIVILEGE
AND POTENTIAL IN
BELONGING TO YOU.
REVEAL YOUR WILL AND
PURPOSE CONCERNING US,
AND THEN GIVE US THE
GRACE TO PURSUE IT WITH
ALL OF OUR HEARTS. WE ASK
THIS IN CHRIST'S NAME,
AMEN.

*Almighty God, Father of all mercies,*

*We thine unworthy servants*

*do give thee most humble and hearty thanks*

> *for all thy goodness and lovingkindness*

> *to us, and to all men;*

*We bless thee for our creation, preservation,*

*and all the blessings of this life;*

*But above all, for thine inestimable love*

> *in the redemption of the world by our Lord Jesus Christ;*

> *for the means of grace, and for the hope of glory.*

*And, we beseech thee,*

> *give us that due sense of all thy mercies,*

> *that our hearts may be unfeignedly thankful,*

> *and that we show forth thy praise*

> *not only with our lips, but in our lives:*

*By giving up ourselves to thy service,*

> *and by walking before thee*

> *in holiness and righteousness all our days;*

*Though Jesus Christ our Lord,*

> *to whom with thee and the Holy Ghost*

> *be all honor and glory, world without end.*

—THE BOOK OF COMMON PRAYER

# DEEPER, NOT WIDER

The things of God have a circumference. They are preserved in a written body of truth. It is like a well—and no one has ever fathomed the depth of God's truth.

To go into the power of the gospel, or of prayer, or the Holy Spirit, or divine love is to plunge ever deeper and deeper into God's well. Every man or woman used by God has gone down into this vast reservoir.

The tendency today, however is merely to splash around in truth for a while . . . and then jump outside the well to the surrounding soil. "Look at this—God is doing a new thing!" people proclaim. In six months or so, of course, the novelty wears off, and they jump again to a new patch of grass. They spend their whole lives hopscotching from one side of God's well to another, never really probing the depth of the living waters inside.

Inside the well there is no cause for leaving or jumping out. Who will ever fathom the fullness of the love of God? Who will ever exhaust the richness of his mercy to fallen human beings? Who will ever understand the real power of prayer?

I kneel before the Father, from whom his whole family in heaven and on earth derives its name. I pray that out of his glorious riches he may strengthen you with power through his Spirit in your inner being, so that Christ may dwell in your hearts through faith. And I pray that you, being rooted and established in love, may have power, together with all the saints, to grasp how wide and long and high and deep is the love of Christ, and to know this love that surpasses knowledge — that you may be filled to the measure of all the fullness of God.

Now to him who is able to do immeasurably
more than all we ask or imagine,
according to his power that is at work
within us, to him be glory in the church
and in Christ Jesus throughout
all generations, for ever and ever! Amen.

—EPHESIANS 3:14–21

*If we prevail in prayer,*
*God will do what only he can do.*

# EARNEST PRAYER

Calvin met Miriam and her two preschoolers when he was just twenty years old. Miriam lived in the apartment two floors below his mother, and she and Calvin warmed to each other right away. Little Monique and Freddy liked the construction worker who made them laugh. Calvin was also something of a weekend musician, playing guitar and singing in nightclubs.

Calvin and Miriam's relationship flourished and even survived a one-year army stint by Calvin that took him away from New York City.

"When I came back home," Calvin admits, "the easiest thing for me to do was just to move in with her. I went back to working road construction, and we had enough money to party through the weekends." The couple eventually added snorting cocaine to their fairly heavy drinking as they and their friends sought new thrills. Then they added marijuana to the mix sometimes even sprinkling the joints with cocaine before rolling them in order to experience both drugs at once.

The live-in arrangement continued with little change, until five years later they wed.

One night the best man from their wedding invited them to a party that featured "freebasing." Not until they left the friend's apartment at 7:30 the next morning, having spent Calvin's entire $720 paycheck for the week, did they realize they had discovered something powerfully attractive—and deadly. They had now joined the world of crack cocaine.

Calvin's obsession with drugs grew ever stronger. If he had any spare cash, it went for crack. If he didn't have cash, he would steal. Some nights he didn't come home at all.

Miriam grew increasingly concerned. What was happening to the man she loved? One night she looked at her two children sleeping innocently in bed while Calvin and his friends were in the kitchen getting high. Moral principles seemed to rise up to warn her of where this was all heading. She promptly threw all the guys out—including Calvin.

At the very time Calvin was deserting the family, Miriam put her faith in Christ. Her spiritual life deepened, and her prayer life increased. She found a church and would openly ask for the prayers of others to bring her husband back from the brink. She simply believed that God would somehow rescue their family.

One day Monique found a flyer announcing a Friday night showing of the film *A Cry for Freedom,* being sponsored by Christ Tabernacle in Queens. The twelve-year-old insisted that Dad go with them to see it. He brushed her off. But later Calvin picked up the flyer from the table and his heart melted enough that he reluctantly agreed to attend the showing.

When the pastor gave an invitation at the end of the film, Calvin was the first one kneeling at the altar. "I didn't actually ask Jesus to come into my heart," he says, "but I was just so guilt-ridden that I had to at least pray and admit the pain I was causing everyone."

The next Sunday, the family returned to church but Calvin still was not willing to get serious about the Lord. By the next weekend he was on the run again. Now the church body began to pray harder for Calvin Hunt's salvation.

Three years went by. Finally, one night—the same night as Christ Tabernacle's weekly prayer meeting—Calvin headed for the family apartment after his wife and children had left for church. Soon he heard a noise. From a closet came the soft sound of someone weeping! Calvin was spooked. He panicked. Running out the door, he dashed three blocks to the train station.

He burst into the church and stood at the back, scanning the crowd. Suddenly the same sounds of crying struck his ears—only much louder than back in the apartment. The whole congregation was in earnest prayer, calling out his name to God in faith! Soon Calvin found himself at the front. The pastor opened his eyes, took one glance—and then gazed upward toward heaven as he said into the microphone, "Thank you, Lord! Thank you, Jesus! Here he is!"

With that, the congregation went absolutely crazy. They had been calling upon the Lord to bring Calvin to himself, and it was happening right before their very eyes.

Falling to his knees, Calvin burst into uncontrollable sobs as he prayed, "O God, I've become everything I said I'd never be. I don't want to die this way. Please come into my life and set me free. Oh, Jesus, I need you so much!"

That summer night in 1988 was the turning point for Calvin Hunt.

Today Calvin no longer wields a jackhammer on the highways of New York City. He has recorded two gospel albums and travels full-time, telling audiences nationwide about the road to God's power in their lives.

Jesus said, "Watch and pray so that you will not fall into temptation. The spirit is willing but the body is weak."

—MATTHEW 26:41

Lord, we beseech you to help and defend us.
Deliver the oppressed, pity the poor.
uplift those who have fallen,
be the portion of those in need,
return to your care those who have gone astray,
feed the hungry, strengthen the weak,
and break the chains of the prisoners.
May all people come to know that you only are God,
that Jesus Christ is your child,
and that we are your people and
the sheep of your pasture.

—CLEMENT OF ROME

When prayer comes from a sincere heart,
it rises into God's presence and stays there.
The more prayers you add,
the more they collect in heaven.
They don't evaporate like a gas.
They remain before God.

Jesus said, "I tell you the truth,
whatever you bind on earth will be bound
in heaven, and whatever you loose on earth
will be loosed in heaven."

—MATTHEW 16:19

*God is drawn to prayer.*

*He delights in communion with us.*

*Prayer releases his blessing into our lives.*


Pressures are exerted all through life to make us want to lie down and quit. The most spiritual person in the world is tempted to get discouraged. I remember seeing a television interview with Billy Graham and his delightfully honest wife, Ruth. The host, David Frost, said something like, "So you two pray together and read the Bible together on a regular basis. But tell me the truth, Mrs. Graham: In all these years of living with Billy, have you never had problems or disagreements? Have you never even once contemplated divorce?"

"Not once," she fired back. "Murder, a few times—but not divorce!"

Obviously, there are challenges to overcome even in the Billy Graham home. You and I have our share of difficulties, but the most important thing is to finish our lives still trusting God.

# TRUE PRAYER

*Prayer ought to enter into the spiritual
habits, but it ceases to be prayer
when it is carried on by habit only. . . .
Desire gives fervor to prayer.
The soul cannot be listless when some great
desire fixes and inflames it. . . .
Strong desires make strong prayers. . . .
The neglect of prayer is the fearful token
of dead spiritual desires.
The soul has turned away from God
when desire after him no longer presses it
into the closet. There can be no true
praying without desire.*

—E. M. BOUNDS

Answer me when I call to you,
O my righteous God.
Give me relief from my distress;
be merciful to me and hear my prayer.

—PSALM 4:1


You are forgiving and good, O Lord,
abounding in love to all who call to you.
Hear my prayer, O LORD;
listen to my cry for mercy.
In the day of my trouble I will call to you
for you will answer me.

—PSALM 86:5-7


Come near to God and he will
come near to you.

—JAMES 4:8

# SEEK THE LORD

Today God's eyes are still running all across America, Canada, Mexico, the islands of the sea, the world . . . looking for someone—anyone—who will totally and passionately seek him, who is determined that every thought and action will be pleasing in his sight. For such a person or group, God will prove himself mighty. His power will explode on their behalf.

When we align ourselves with the channel of God's living grace, all kinds of marvelous things take place. His power energizes us to face any army, large or small, and win victories for him. We call upon him, and he sends us forth to accomplish what we could never do alone, regardless of our money, education, or track record.

Anything and everything is possible with God if we approach him with a broken spirit. We must humble ourselves, get rid of the debris in our lives, and keep leaning on him instead of our own understanding. Your future and mine are determined by this one thing: seeking after the Lord. The blessings we receive and then pass along to others all hang on this truth: "he rewards those who earnestly see him" (Hebrews 11:6).

*Persistent calling upon the Lord*
*breaks through every stronghold of the devil,*
*for nothing is impossible with God.*

Seek the Lord while he may be found;
call on him while he is near.
Let the wicked forsake his way
and the evil man his thoughts.
Let him turn to the Lord, and he will have
mercy on him, and
to our God, for he will freely pardon.

—ISAIAH 55:6–7

God, you are with me
and you can help me;
You were with me when I was taken,
and you are with me now.
You strengthen me.

The God I serve is everywhere—
in heaven and earth and the sea,
But he is above them all,
for all live in him:
All were created by him,
and by him only do they remain.

I will worship only the true God;
you will I carry in my heart;
No one on earth shall be able to
separate me from you.

—QUIRINUS OF SISCIA

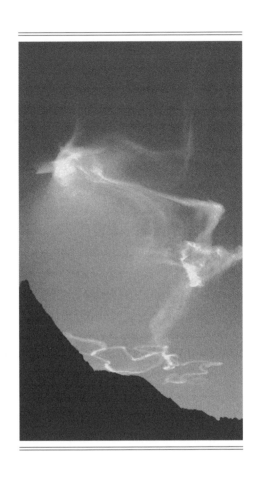

*Communion with God*

*is our greatest need.*

# THE LORD'S PRAYER

"This, then, is how you should pray:

"'Our Father in heaven,

hallowed be your name,

your kingdom come,

your will be done

on earth as it is in heaven.

Give us today our daily bread.

Forgive us our debts,

as we also have forgiven our debtors.

And lead us not into temptation,

but deliver us from the evil one.'"

—MATTHEW 6:9–13

We are in the habit of praying for trivial and insignificant things. When we pray, we don't take into account the great majesty of God. If God wanted to give us only petty and superficial things, he wouldn't have given us such a magnificent model for prayer: "Our Father in heaven, let your name be kept holy. Let your kingdom come ..." God has plenty of resources, and he's not a tightwad. He generously offers us the best gifts available in heaven and on earth. He expects that we will ask him for many things and that we will sincerely believe that we will get what we request.

*When we receive what we ask for in the Lord's Prayer, we are, in effect, receiving heaven and earth and everything they contain. For when we ask for God's name to be kept holy, for his kingdom to come, and for his will to be done, we are overpowering countless devils and engulfing the whole world with one prayer.*

—MARTIN LUTHER

Do not be anxious about anything,

but in everything, by prayer

and petition, with thanksgiving,

present your requests to God.

—PHILIPPIANS 4:6

# GETTING WHAT WE NEED

God's grace goes further and deeper than we can ever imagine. God alone can give us what we really need: a pure heart, a steadfast and willing spirit. No matter how deep and dark the secret, no matter how many times a certain sin has defeated you; God can bring change to your life. But it must be his Holy Spirit working from within and not your weak attempts to "do better the next time." All God asks of you is to bring the whole, sorry mess to him so he can begin the spiritual transformation you need.

*The sins of my entire life,*
*by which I have so often offended you,*
*my God, weigh me down like a mountain*
*of my own making.*
*I wonder, 'What will be the end*
*of all this'?*
*Yet, I do not lose hope.*

*I cannot bear this alone;*
*I know I am weak.*
*But your strength will keep*
*me from falling.*
*The prayers of others will*
*uphold me in my time of need.*
*I cannot repay such mercy;*
*to offer my life is only right.*

—JOHN RI

# FINDING GOD'S WILL

Many people today are making decisions without a passing thought of seeking God. They think that as long as they don't lie, kill, steal, or commit adultery they are in the will of God. They proceed to make other important life decisions based on common sense — or sometimes even less than that. Just "I felt like it!" "My friends are doing it." "My world calls this 'success.'"

When we leave God out of these decisions, we are not really walking in faith. Instead of tapping into God's great resources of wisdom, we rely on mere human ideas.

Isn't it silly to think that the God who gave his own Son for us doesn't also care about the details of our lives?

A faith-filled believer will pray earnestly until he finds God's will for things such as

> - *Changing jobs*
> - *Dealing with a difficult child*
> - *Choosing a school for your children*
> - *Moving*
> - *Which believer to marry*
> - *Buying a home*
> - *Joining a ministry in the church.*

The all-knowing Creator of the universe wants to show us the way in these matters. He has a plan for where we belong and where we don't belong. Therefore we need to seek his direction.

*God can do more in one day*
*than we can accomplish in ten years*
*of human effort. I have spent months*
*laboring to push doors open*
*that only God could release, and*
*I am still learning that far more*
*is accomplished by persevering in prayer*
*than in taking charge of things myself.*

"For I know the plans I have for you,"
declares the LORD, "plans to prosper you and
not to harm you, plans to give you hope and a
future. Then you will call upon me and come
and pray to me, and I will listen to you. You
will seek me and find me when you seek me
with all your heart."

—JEREMIAH 29:11-13

I want to affirm that God is not dead; he really does communicate today. He's interested in every part of your life, your home, your finances, every kind of decision—and more than just the moral issues. His eye is always on you. He wants to lead you. But you have to believe that he will indeed speak to you when you wait before him in believing prayer, with a yielded heart to do his will.

God knows things we have no way of knowing. When we don't inquire of the Lord and ask in faith for guidance, we totally miss what he wants to accomplish.

# EMERGENCY PRAYERS

Learning to pray when there's an emergency or when something is frightening us requires a lot of discipline. Instead of praying we tend to torture ourselves with anxiety and worry. All we can think about is trying to get rid of the problem.

The devil often tricks us when temptation or suffering first begins, whether dealing with spiritual or physical matters. He immediately barges in and makes us so upset about the problem that we become consumed by it. In this way, he tears us away from praying. He makes us so confused that we don't even think about praying. When we finally begin to pray, we have already tortured ourselves half to death. The devil knows what prayer can accomplish. That's why he creates so many obstacles and makes it so inconvenient for us that we never get around to prayer.

*You should get into the habit of falling on your knees and spreading out your needs in front of God the moment you have an emergency or become frightened. Prayer is the very best medicine there is. It always works and never fails—if you would just use it!*

—MARTIN LUTHER

Prayers of intercession are the sound of people freely expressing their heart's needs, desires, and praises. David Jeremiah described it not as a mechanical exercise, but a real calling out to God with passion for my need. Far from being a new invention, this kind of prayer has ancient roots. It goes back before Christ, before David, even before Moses organized a formal worship with the tabernacle. There are countless times in the Old Testament when people called upon God; cried out to God to implore his aid. This is the essence of true prayer that touches God.

Charles Spurgeon once remarked that "the best style of prayer is that which cannot be called anything else but a cry."

Isn't that what God invites us to do all through the Bible? God is not aloof. He is not disconnected. He says continually through the centuries, "I'll help you, I really will. When you don't know where to turn, then turn to me. When you're ready to throw up your hands—throw them up to me. Put your voice behind them, too and I'll come and help you."

# FRESH PRAISE

Satan's main strategy with God's people has always been to whisper, "Don't call, don't ask, don't depend on God to do great things. You'll get along fine if you just rely on your own cleverness and energy." The truth of the matter is that the devil is not terribly frightened of our human efforts and credentials. But he knows his kingdom will be damaged when we lift up our hearts to God.

God desires praise from our lives . . . but the only way fresh praise and honor will come is if we keep coming to him in times of need and difficulty. Then he will intervene to show himself strong on our behalf, and we will know that he has done it.

Are not we all prone to be a little cocky and think we can handle things just fine? But let some trouble come, and how quickly we sense our inadequacy. Trouble is one of God's great servants because it reminds us how much we continually need the Lord. Otherwise, we tend to forget about entreating him. For some reason we want to carry on by ourselves.

What other nation is so great as to have
their gods near them the way the Lord our
God is near us whenever we pray to him?

—DEUTERONOMY 4:7

This is what the Lord says, he who
made the earth, the Lord who formed it
and established it—the Lord is his name:
"Call to me and I will answer you and
tell you great and unsearchable things
you do not know."

—JEREMIAH 33:2-3

*"Call upon me in the day of trouble;*
*I will deliver you, and you will honor me,"*
*says the LORD.*

—PSALM 50:15

*Suffer me never to think that I have*

*knowledge enough to need no teaching,*

*wisdom enough to need no correction,*

*talents enough to need no grace,*

*goodness enough to need no progress,*

*humility enough to need no repentance,*

*devotion enough to need no quickening,*

*strength sufficient without thy Spirit;*

*lest, standing still, I fall back for evermore.*

—ERIC MILNER-WHITE

Whatever you do, keep seeking God's will for your life. He will do it! Don't settle for anything less. Wait for God—he knows how to give you the best!

"My house will be called a house of

prayer," says the LORD.

— ISAIAH 56:7

# THE POWER
## OF PRAYERS
### OF THE
## CHURCH

# SERIOUS PRAYER

One of the distinguishing traits of the early church was their practice of serious prayer. The apostles never said, "Lord, teach us to preach" or "Lord, teach us to lead worship." But they *had* asked, "Lord, teach us to pray" (Luke 11:1). Something about Jesus' ability to commune with his Father in heaven fascinated them.

When the Holy Spirit was poured out upon them, he birthed a new spirit of prayer and intercession. They began following a simple practice: The best thing to do whenever emergencies come is to gather to pray! It was a living reality to them that God responds when people call upon his name. Indeed, this faith and fervency was begotten by the Spirit of God.

*Prayer is the avenue God*
*uses to come and bless his people.*

# BEGINNING THE YEAR

Every first week of January we shut down the normal schedule at the Brooklyn Tabernacle for a series of nightly prayer meetings. No other activities or programs go on that week because we know all too well that we must be strong in the Lord for whatever challenges or satanic attacks the New Year might hold. The building is filled to overflowing each night with people seeking the Lord and waiting in his presence.

The next week we return to our regular rhythm of ongoing Tuesday night prayer meetings plus the other classes and activities. Our Prayer Band, headed by Associate Pastor Ken Ware, has a rotating contingent in our building interceding at the throne of grace twenty-four hours a day, seven days a week, with no interruption. At certain times during the year we have also opened up the church in the late afternoons for corporate prayer after work.

Having said all this, I must still admit that our church needs a fresh visitation of God's Spirit, and all our leadership knows it. Yes, we thank God for his blessings, the evidence of his grace all around us. But there is so much more to receive from him. We are just scratching the surface of what we know God can and will do in and through us.

They went upstairs to the room
where they were staying. Those present
were Peter, John, James and Andrew;
Philip and Thomas, Bartholomew and
Matthew; James son of Alphaeus and Simon
the Zealot, and Judas son of James.
They all joined together constantly in prayer,
along with the women and Mary
the mother of Jesus, and with his brothers.

—ACTS 1:13–14

# AN EASY RESPONSIBILITY

Believers don't view prayer as hard work, but as a responsibility that is easy to fulfill. They pray in faith because they know God has promised to hear them. They pray from the heart, revealing their agony and needs. They pray with groans and sighs, as Paul says, "The Spirit intercedes along with our groans that cannot be expressed in words" (Romans 8:26, *GOD'S WORD*). The Spirit knows that God is listening to him and that excessive rambling isn't necessary.

*Elijah, Elisha, David, and others in the Old Testament used few words when they prayed and came straight to the point. The fathers in the early church said it well, "Nothing will be accomplished by long-winded prayers." In fact, the church fathers recommended short, whispered expressions of sorrow and prayers consisting of only a word or two. This kind of praying can be done anytime, even when reading, writing, or doing other tasks. God doesn't want long, drawn-out prayers. Instead, he wants sincere prayers that flow out of a faithful heart.*

—MARTIN LUTHER

Only turning God's house into a house of fervent prayer will reverse the power of evil so evident in the world today.

*I pray God that the church may be preserved immovable and steadfast in the true faith.*

—MARTIN, BISHOP OF ROME

# CONFIRMATION
## FROM GOD

It is not a sign of weakness to look for confirmation and validation of your sense of God's will as you inquire of the Lord. It is often a good idea, in fact, to get a prayer partner or call a pastor who can validate your sense of God's message.

When I first heard about a four-thousand-seat theater in downtown Brooklyn that was for sale and might possibly solve our church's space problems, I got excited. Even though the building was in terrible shape and would require millions of dollars for restoration, I could see the potential for this to become the new Brooklyn Tabernacle.

Very quickly, however, I said to my associate pastors, "You go see it for yourselves and then pray. Unless all six of you feel that God is leading us this way we won't even present it to the congregation." Would God hide such an important matter from my fellow leaders and reveal it only to me? I don't think so. I also brought other ministers whom I respect, such as David Wilkerson, to see the building. I wanted confirmation that God was leading us this way.

In time, we felt an agreement in our spirits that this step was right. Although the price tag was huge, we moved ahead in faith and confidence.

[The believers] devoted themselves to the
apostles' teaching and to the fellowship,
to the breaking of bread and to prayer.

—ACTS 2:42

This is the confidence we have in approaching
God: that if we ask anything according to
his will, he hears us. And if we know that
he hears us—whatever we ask—we know
that we have what we asked of him.

—1 JOHN 5:14–15

If any of you lacks wisdom, he should ask
God, who gives generously to all without
finding fault, and it will be given to him.
But when he asks, he must believe and not
doubt, because he who doubts is like a wave
of the sea, blown and tossed by the wind.

—JAMES 1:5–6

# PERSEVERE IN PRAYER

When we seek God for answers, we must persevere in prayer, letting it build up day after day until the force of it becomes a mighty tide pushing over all obstacles. No wonder God says his house is supposed to be known as a house of prayer—not merely a house of preaching or of singing, but especially of prayer. How else will we receive great answers from God unless we persevere in prayer?

If we call upon the Lord, he has promised in his Word to answer, to bring the unsaved to himself, to pour out his Spirit among us. If we don't call upon the Lord, he has promised nothing—nothing at all. It's as simple as that. No matter what I preach or what we claim to believe in our heads, the future will depend upon our times of prayer.

The format of a prayer meeting is not nearly as important as its essence—touching the Almighty, crying out with one's whole being. I have been in noisy prayer meetings that were mainly a show. I have been with groups in times of silent prayer that were deeply spiritual. The atmosphere of the meeting may vary; what matters most is that we encounter the God of the universe, not just each other.

*Good God, may we confess your name*
*to the end;*
*May we emerge unmarked and glorious*
*from the traps and darkness of this world.*
*As you have bound us together*
*by charity and peace,*
*And as together we have persevered*
*under persecution,*
*So may we also rejoice together*
*in your heavenly kingdom.*

—CYPRIAN OF CARTHAGE

*God still uses foolish tools in the hands*
*of weak people to build his kingdom.*
*Backed by prayer and his power,*
*we can accomplish the unthinkable.*

# THE PRAYER BAND

The Brooklyn Tabernacle Choir sings a song that captures God's penchant for using the weak to shame the strong. It goes, "If you can use anything, Lord, you can use me." Kenneth Ware, one of the associate pastors, has shown this kind of faith more than once. Years ago, this godly, gray-haired African American started all-night prayer meetings on Friday nights in the church. Then he organized a Prayer Band—a group of people committed to calling on the Lord at the church on a continuing schedule.

Soon the members of the Prayer Band were praying five nights a week, from 11 P.M. to 6 A.M. Today they are in the church seven days a week, twenty-four hours a day, praying in three-hour shifts or longer. Every request we receive is written on a little card and lifted to the Lord for the next thirty days.

I remember the day Pastor Ware said to me in a fatherly tone (he's at least fifteen years older than I am), "Pastor, you know, we're still not seeing God do all he wants to do. You're preaching with all your heart, but we need to see more conviction of sin, more of God's manifest presence in our services."

I agreed and listened, wondering what he would say next.

"I'm serious," Pastor Ware continued. "We probably have half a dozen HIV-positive people in every meeting. We've got crack addicts. We've got marriages on the rocks, brokenhearted moms, young people hardened by the city. They really need the Lord."

"I want to have the Prayer Band start praying somewhere about this during the actual meetings, while you're preaching. We need to see God break through among us."

I gave Pastor Ware my blessing, and to this day he has twenty or so people closed in a room to pray during each of the four meetings—a total of eighty intercessors each Sunday. They start by praying with the pastors fifteen minutes before the meeting and keep going even after everything ends. Sometimes, in leaving the building at ten or ten-thirty at night, I have heard them still praying.

Praying the Lord's Prayer every day
is certainly a worthwhile habit,
especially for ordinary people and children.
We can pray it in the morning,
in the evening, and at the dinner table
—at any time for that matter.
As we pray this prayer together,
we bring our needs before God.
God the Father wants us to trust
that he will meet our needs.
We are overjoyed to be his children
through Christ.
And so, because we trust that he will
give us what he promised,
we can pray to him with confidence,
in the name of Christ, our Lord.

—MARTIN LUTHER

# AMALIA'S STORY

I grew up in the Smith Projects on the Lower East Side. I was the third of seven children packed into an apartment on the sixteenth floor. My father was a kitchen worker in one of the big hotels; he and my mother had both come from Puerto Rico. My father was an alcoholic and made our lives miserable. My parents would argue a lot about money. Even though there wasn't enough money for the necessities, there was definitely money for alcohol. And that only made the fights worse. When I would see my father hitting my mother and pushing her around, I would just run to my room and seethe with anger.

I was about nine years old the first time I stood up to my father. In the middle of the yelling, I said to him one night, "If you hurt my mother, I'm going to kill you!" I tuned to my mother and continued, "Look—you go sleep in my bed to get away from him, and I'll sleep in yours." I thought I was helping the situation. But that was the biggest mistake of my life—because that night, my father began to molest me.

Soon the next household fight came along—now what was I going to do? I told myself I should try again to protect my mom; maybe it would be different this time.

It was not. An ugly pattern began to be set. Before long, it started looking as if my father was actually starting arguments with my mom in order to get us to switch for the night. Or he would just openly call from his room, "Come in here, Amalia. I want you in here with me."

With all this going on at home, school was an ordeal for me. I couldn't concentrate. I was numb inside. This went on for years, until I was sixteen and was eagerly plotting to get out of the house. For me the escape route was a boy named Richard. We soon found a minister to marry us and had a big Puerto Rican reception. Richard had a job at Metropolitan Hospital, and I figured he would take care of me from now on; I didn't really need to finish high school.

Richard introduced me to drugs, starting with pot. I realized it could make me forget all my problems at least for a while. Then came LSD and cocaine. I wanted anything I took to lift me up and make me happy.

The marriage lasted little more than a year. I got involved with one man after another, trying to stay high twenty-four hours a day. I was now in my mid-twenties, and all this fast living just wasn't as great as I thought it would be. I decided I should get a steady line of work. When I applied at a place in Midtown they offered to hire me as a barmaid. Not until I reported for work did I realize what the tiny stage in the center of the bar was for. This was in fact a topless go-go bar.

My first time on stage was nerve-wracking. In fact, I probably couldn't have done it if I hadn't gotten high to start with. But as minutes went by and the customers started cheering and throwing money my way, I saw the benefits of this line of work. Then one night right in the middle of a dance, I passed out—collapsed right there on stage.

I figured I had had too many Black Russian drinks that night. But the real cause was, I was pregnant. I'd been pregnant before and had always gotten abortions. But this time it was different. For some reason, I wanted to go ahead and see what having a baby would be like.

I had to humble myself and ask my mother if I could move back home. She took me in. We got into a big fight. Underneath, I think I was still mad at her for what happened years before.

In time, I gave birth to a healthy baby boy, whom I named Vinny.

Once, after another argument with my mother, I went up on the roof of our building. I thought about the lousy job of mothering I was doing. Maybe I should just jump. I was scared to do it, but I was more scared to go on living.

A couple of weeks ago, Mickey, my sister's husband, invited my mother and some of the rest of us to come with him here to your church. When you got up there to preach and started to speak about God's love, I listened. I remember you saying something about "Jesus loves you no matter what you've done. He will forgive you and take you past whatever has been done to you in your life." When you asked people to come to the front for prayer, I got up and went with the rest.

*Amalia told me later that when she went home that night to her mother, she exclaimed, "Mom, guess what I did tonight! I gave my heart to Jesus Christ, and he saved me! He cleansed me! I'm not the same anymore."*

*A few years after her salvation, Amalia met a dental technician in our church, and they fell in love and were married. The Lord gave them a son together, a half brother to Vinny, and the family moved in 1987 to another state. There they continue today to walk with God worshiping and serving in a church.*

*God likes to see his people shut up to this,*

*that there is no hope but in prayer.*

*Herein lies the Church's power against the world.*

—ANDREW BONAR

# THE INSTINCT TO PRAY

Let's not play games with ourselves. Let's not divert attention away from the weak prayer life of our own churches. In Acts 4, when the apostles were unjustly arrested, imprisoned, and threatened, they didn't call for a protest; they didn't reach for some political leverage. Instead, they headed to a prayer meeting. Soon the place was vibrating with the power of the Holy Spirit.

The apostles had this instinct: When in trouble, pray. When intimidated pray. When challenged, pray. When persecuted, pray.

*Let everyone who is godly pray to you*
*while you may be found;*
*surely when the mighty waters rise,*
*they will not reach him.*

—PSALM 32:6

On their release, Peter and John went back
to their own people and reported all
that the chief priests and elders had said
to them. When they heard this,
they raised their voices in prayer to God.

—ACTS 4:24

After [the believers] prayed, the place
where they were meeting was shaken.
And they were all filled with the Holy Spirit
and spoke the word of God boldly.

—ACTS 4:31

The Bible does say,
"My house shall be called
a house of prayer for all nations."
Preaching, music, the reading of the Word—
these things are fine;
I believe in and practice all of them.
But they must never override prayer
as the defining mark of God's dwelling.
The honest truth is that
I have seen God do more in people's lives
during ten minutes of real prayer
than in ten of my sermons.

# REVIVING PASSIONATE PRAYER

Revivals have never been dominated by eloquent or clever preaching. If you had timed the meetings with a stopwatch, you would have found far more minutes given to prayer, weeping, and repentance than to sermons. In the "Prayer Meeting Revival" of 1857-59 there was virtually no preaching at all. Yet it apparently produced the greatest harvest of any spiritual awakening in American history: estimates run to 1,000,000 converts across the United States, out of a national population at that time of only 30,000,000. That would be proportionate to 9,000,000 Americans today falling on their knees in repentance!

How did this happen? A quiet businessman named Jeremiah Lanphier started a Wednesday noon prayer meeting in a Dutch Reformed church here in New York City, no more than a quarter mile from Wall Street. The first week, six people showed up. The next week, twenty came. The next week, forty... and they decided to have daily meetings instead.

"There was no fanaticism, no hysteria, just an incredible movement of people to pray," reports J. Edwin Orr. "The services were not given over to preaching. Instead anyone was free to pray."

During the fourth week, the financial Panic of 1857 hit; the bond market crashed, and the first banks failed. (Within a month, more than 1,400 banks had collapsed.) People began calling out to God more seriously than ever. Lanphier's church started having three noontime prayer meetings in different rooms. John Street Methodist Church, a few doors east of Broadway, was packed out as well. Soon Burton's Theater on Chambers Street was jammed with 3,000 people each noon.

The scene was soon replicated in Boston, New Haven, Philadelphia, Washington, and the South. By the next spring 2,000 Chicagoans were gathering each day in the Metropolitan Theater to pray. A young 21-year-old in those meetings, newly arrived in the city, felt his first call to do Christian work. He wrote his mother back East that he was going to start a Sunday school class. His name was Dwight L. Moody.

Does anyone really think that America today is lacking preachers, books, Bible translations, and neat doctrinal statements? What we really lack is the passion to call upon the Lord until he opens the heavens and shows himself powerful.

*Hear us, O God, the Father of our*
*Lord Jesus Christ.*
*Through your name the sea is calmed,*
*the fire is quenched and the grave*
*and death are brought to nothing;*
*You comfort those who are oppressed,*
*you heal those who are suffering;*
*Those who are lost in the sea*
*you come to their aid;*
*In like manner, my Lord, also come*
*to help us and deliver us from this time;*
*For you are the true God,*
*the help of those who are oppressed*
*and in tribulation*
*and yours is the power and the glory forever.*
*Amen.*

—SHENOUFE THE COPT

*Christians meet to seek the Lord,*
*and then somehow, some way,*
*the gospel begins to spread in power,*
*changing lives wherever it goes.*

*We must go back quickly to God's*
*pattern for revival, blessing,*
*and successful evangelism.*
*We must return to prayer,*
*not only personal and private*
*but also corporate and public.*
*God has promised us all*
*an abundant supply of the Spirit—*
*rivers, floods, and oceans—rather than*
*trying to live off meager drops now*
*and again from his fountain.*

# OUTREACH BORN
# IN PRAYER

At the Brooklyn Tabernacle a few years ago, we saw the Lord break through to an equally tough sinner in answer to believing prayer. The whole outreach that touched Ricardo Aparicio was born in prayer. We have learned over the years to let God birth something in people who are spiritually sensitive, who begin to pray and feel a calling.

A fellow named Terry and some others grew concerned for the subculture of male prostitutes that flourishes on the Lower West Side of Manhattan in a place called the "salt mine," where the city keeps salt for deicing streets in the winter. Many of them, as boys, were raped by adult male relatives. Our outreach team began to bring food and blankets during the daylight hours on Saturday when the men weren't distracted by their "work." Although the men made considerable money, they tended to squander it on drugs. That left them scavenging garbage cans and dumpsters for food. To feel compassion for these guys, to understand their wretched life, was extremely difficult. We prayed fervently on Tuesday nights for love, compassion—and protection.

One Sunday afternoon about half an hour before the afternoon service, Terry knocked on my office door. "Pastor Cymbala! We've got twenty-seven guys here today from the 'salt mines.' Isn't that great!"

The congregation took their presence in stride, even though the men didn't exactly look — or smell — All-American. At the end of the service some of them responded to give their hearts to the Lord. Others sat stunned as church members greeted them with smiles and handshakes.

Walking down the center aisle, I bumped into an attractive woman in a black dress with blond, shoulder-length hair, nicely done nails, black stockings, and high heels. "Excuse me, ma'am," I said.

She turned . . . and this low voice with a heavy Spanish accent replied, "No, that's okay, man."

My heart skipped a beat. This was not a woman after all. But neither was it a sloppy transvestite. This was a knockout of a "woman."

His name was Ricardo, known on the street as "Sarah." Ricardo had been plying his trade for at least ten years, and the dreariness was finally starting to get to him. He sat in the meeting and it dawned on him that maybe he could be different. But the idea that God was stronger, that God could in fact change him on the inside...that was a new thought. Ricardo kept listening, and after about a month, he gave his heart to the Lord. It was not a dramatic conversion: I am not even sure when it happened. But it was real on the inside.

Ricardo eventually moved to Texas. A few years later, at Christmastime, while I was in my office just as the Sunday afternoon service was beginning, I received a message that said Ricardo was dying.

He wanted to talk to me. I heard a fragile, wispy voice. I prepared to make a comforting little speech, to tell him he would be going to heaven soon, that he would get there before me but I would see him on the other side for all eternity. . . .

The Holy Spirit stopped me. No! a voice seemed to say. Fight for him! Cry out to me!

I began to intercede with intensity, fighting against the death that loomed before him. "O God, touch Ricardo with your power! This is not his time to die. Restore him, for your glory, I pray."

When I finished, I marched directly into the meeting and stopped it. "I've just gotten off the phone with Ricardo. He's very sick with AIDS— but I want us to pray for his recovery."

That unleashed a torrent of prayer as people cried out to God for Ricardo.

Within three weeks, Ricardo actually flew to New York and came walking unannounced into a Tuesday night prayer meeting. The crowd gasped with joy.

In my heart I felt that God spared him for a reason: To get his testimony onto video so that others could know his remarkable story.

The last time I saw Ricardo, a year later his weight had dropped again. "I'm so tired," he said. "I've fought this disease long enough; I just want to go to Jesus. I can go now, because you have me on film, and everybody will know in years to come what Jesus did in my life." He passed away not long afterward.

Ricardo's story is evidence of what God will do in response to fervent prayer. No one is beyond his grace. No situation anywhere on earth is too hard for God.

## GOD'S GOODNESS

*No one receives anything from God*
*because of the quality of the prayer,*
*but only because of God's goodness.*
*God anticipates all of our requests and*
*desires. With his promise, he prompts us*
*to pray and desire these things so that*
*we will learn how much he cares for us.*
*He cares for us so much that he is prepared*
*to give us even more than we are ready to*
*receive or to ask for. Because he is offering us*
*so much, we can pray with confidence.*

—MARTIN LUTHER

Jesus said, "So I say to you:
Ask and it will be given to you;
seek and you will find; knock and the door
will be opened to you. For everyone who asks
receives; he who seeks finds; and to him
who knocks, the door will be opened."

—LUKE 11:9–10

Surely you will find delight in the Almighty
and will lift up your face to God.
You will pray to him, and he will hear you.

—JOB 22:26–27

# BUILDING A CHURCH

By 1977 more people were trying to fit into the pews on Sunday morning and Sunday night than there was room for. Down the block was a YWCA with an auditorium that could seat 400 to 500 people. We were able to rent it on Sundays. Meeting in the YWCA was a temporary solution, at best, to the overcrowding. We purchased a lot across the street in the hope of one day erecting a real church building. It required a big step of faith, but God provided the funds.

We scheduled a groundbreaking ceremony, excited about starting a new building, a permanent home. Would you believe that on that special Sunday, it rained so hard we couldn't go outdoors to put a shovel in the ground? Disappointed, we packed ourselves back into the YMCA auditorium that evening.

But in that meeting God clearly spoke to us that it wasn't the ground across the street he wanted to break. Instead he would break our hearts and build his church on that foundation.

The downpour, as it turned out, was providential. A few months later, a large 1,400 seat theater on Flatbush Avenue, the main north-south artery of Brooklyn, became available for only $150,000.

We were able to sell the lot at a profit. We needed to sell the run-down Atlantic Avenue building as well in order to buy the theater. Some pastors came to look at our old place and appeared serious about buying it. We agreed on a price — only to find out later they hadn't even tried to secure a mortgage. By then we were in danger of losing our option on the theater.

All our dreams were about to come crashing down. At a Tuesday night prayer meeting we laid the problem before God, weeping and pleading for a last-minute rescue of some kind.

On Wednesday afternoon the doorbell at the church rang. I went downstairs to answer. There stood a well-dressed stranger, who, it turned out, was a Kuwaiti businessman. He walked in and looked around while I held my breath.

"What are you asking for this building?" he said at last.

I cleared my throat and answered weakly, "Ninety-five thousand."

He paused a moment and then said, "That's fair. We have a deal."

"Uh, well, how long will it take you to make arrangements at the bank?" I was still worried that our option on the Flatbush property would expire before we could close this deal.

"No bank, nothing," he answered abruptly. "Just get your lawyer to call my lawyer — here's the name and phone number. Cash deal." And with that, he was gone.

Once again, our prayer had been answered in a surprising way.

God had formed a core of people who wanted to pray, who believed that nothing was too big for him to handle. No matter what roadblock we faced, no matter what attack came against us, no matter how wild the city became in the late seventies—as cocaine arrived on top of heroin, and then crack cocaine on top of that—God could still change people and deliver them from evil. He was building his church in a tough neighborhood, and as long as people kept calling out for his blessing and help, he had fully committed himself to respond.

Jesus said, "Therefore I tell you, whatever you ask for in prayer, believe that you have received it, and it will be yours."

—MARK 11:24

# DRIVEN TO PRAY

Prayer cannot truly be taught by principles and seminars and symposiums. It has to be born out of a whole environment of felt need. If I say, "I ought to pray," I will soon run out of motivation and quit; the flesh is too strong. I have to be driven to pray.

Yes, the roughness of inner-city life has pressed us to pray. When you have alcoholics trying to sleep on the back steps of your building, when your teenagers are getting assaulted and knifed on the way to youth meetings, when you bump into transvestites in the lobby after church, you can't escape your need for God. According to a recent Columbia University study, twenty-one cents of every dollar New Yorkers pay in city taxes is spent trying to cope with the effects of smoking, drinking, and drug abuse.

But is the rest of the country coasting along in fine shape? I think not. In the smallest village in the Farm Belt, there are still urgent needs. Every congregation has wayward kids, family members who aren't serving God. Do we really believe that God can bring them back to himself?

Too many Christians live in a state of denial: "Well, I hope my child will come around someday." Some parents have actually given up: "I guess nothing can be done. Bobby didn't turn out right—but we tried; we dedicated him to the Lord when he as a baby. Maybe someday. . . ."

The more we pray, the more we sense our need to pray. And the more we sense a need to pray, the more we want to pray.

*The eternal kingdom is within sight,*
*a kingdom that shall suffer no loss.*
*Lord Jesus Christ, we are Christians*
*we are your servants;*
*You alone are our hope,*
*the hope of all Christians.*
*God almighty, God most high:*
*we give you praise,*
*we give praise to your name.*

—THELICA OF ABITINE

We all have the same spirit,

and this is what unites us in our actions

and all that we do together.

This is the bond of love that puts evil to flight

and that which is most pleasing to God;

It is by our praying together

that we receive what we ask.

These are the ties that link our hearts together,

and make mere mortals the children of God.

To inherit your kingdom, O God,

we must be your children;

To be your children,

we must love one another.

—MONTANUS AND HIS COMPANIONS

# PRAYING IN A TIME OF NEED

No matter what you or I have been taught, no matter what church setting we have experienced, we see that prayer in the early church was apparently a very vocal, very earnest thing. But then again, David had showed much the same emotion: "I cried out to God for help; I cried out to God to hear me. When I was in distress, I sought the Lord; at night I stretched out untiring hands" (Psalm 77:1–2). So this kind of praying was not new to God's people.

Too many times when we are under stress or opposition, we do everything but call a prayer meeting. We try to pull political levers, we hold strategy sessions, we "claim the promises" in a rote sort of way instead of praying them biblically. But God said we could "receive mercy and find grace to help us in our time of need." Where? At "the throne of grace" (Hebrews 4:16).

The root problem is the need for the Holy Spirit to come in power and birth a true spirit of prayer. In other words, we must first secure the Spirit's presence and grace; then we can move out in powerful praying for all kinds of other needs. Let us remember the Lord's promise: "If you then, though you are evil, know how to give good gifts to your children, how much more will your Father in heaven give the Holy Spirit to those who ask him!" (Luke 11:13).

Jesus said, "The harvest is plentiful but the workers are few. Ask the Lord of the harvest, therefore, to send out workers into his harvest field" (Matthew 9:37–38). In our churches today we have lots of critics and lots of people who like to discuss things — but not too many workers. Notice, though, that the directive is to pray that the Lord of the harvest will raise up and identify needed laborers.

# ACCOMPLISHING
# GREAT THINGS

The water of God's Spirit is absolutely free, but we must wait by faith continually to receive fresh infillings of this promise from the Father. This is how Luke ends his gospel narrative as he records Jesus' last words to his disciples: "I am going to send you what my Father has promised; but stay in the city until you have been clothed with power from on high" (Luke 24:49).

Two thousand years later, this is still the greatest need of the Christian church—to wait regularly in seasons of corporate and individual prayer until we are "clothed with power from on high." These are the garments Jesus will still give his people—supernatural ability, might, and power from the Holy Spirit so we can accomplish great things for God's glory.

*It is not through human talent*
*or earthly resources that*
*the true Christian church is built,*
*but rather through men and women*
*saturated with God's spirit*
*and full of his Word.*

Be joyful in hope,

patient in affliction,

faithful in prayer.

— ROMANS 12:12

# THE POWER
## OF PRAYERS
## OF FAITH

## PRAYER OF FAITH

Is any one of you in trouble? He should pray.
Is anyone happy? Let him sing songs of praise.
Is any one of you sick? He should call the
elders of the church to pray over him and
anoint him with oil in the name of the Lord.
And the prayer offered in faith will make the
sick person well; the Lord will raise him up.
If he has sinned, he will be forgiven.
Therefore confess your sins to each other
and pray for each other so that you may
be healed. The prayer of a righteous man is
powerful and effective.

– JAMES 5:13–16

# WHAT IS FAITH?

What is faith? It is total dependence upon God that becomes supernatural in its working. People with faith develop a second kind of sight. They see more than just the circumstances; they see God, right beside them. Can they prove it? No. But by faith they know he's there nonetheless.

Without faith, says Hebrews 11:6, it is *impossible* to please God. Nothing else counts if faith is missing. There is no other foundation for Christian living, no matter the amount of self-effort or energy spent. Nothing else touches the Father's heart as much as when his children simply trust him wholeheartedly.

I meet people who at one time would pray over anything and everything! Even if they lost their glasses, they would pray to find them—and amazingly, the glasses would show up. Now the same people seem not to believe that God can do much of anything.

Oh, they will still give you the standard confession of faith: "Yes, I have faith in the God who answers prayer." But that vibrant trust and expectation are no more. They aren't saying, "Come on—let's go after this problem in the name of the Lord."

*We should pray with confidence, knowing that*
*God will answer our requests without delay.*
*It's impossible for sincere, persistent prayer to*
*remain unheard. But because we don't believe,*
*we aren't persistent enough and don't*
*experience God's goodness and help.*
*So we must become more enthusiastic about*
*faith and prayer, knowing that God is pleased*
*when we persevere. In fact, God ordered us*
*to be persistent in prayer: "Ask, and you will*
*receive. Search, and you will find. Knock, and*
*the door will be opened for you" (Matthew 7:7).*

– MARTIN LUTHER

God will give you whatever you ask.

– JOHN 11:22

# DEEP FAITH

Some years ago I was taking my granddaughter Susie on a walk when a couple of homeless men came walking toward us. Their scruffy appearance made her afraid. In her little mind, she thought she was about to be harmed. She was already holding my hand, but instantly I felt her push her body into mine as she grabbed onto my pant leg. "Papa!" she whispered. Of course, I put my arm around her and said that everything was going to be all right. The men passed us on the sidewalk without incident.

Inside, my heart was brimming. That instantaneous reflex of reaching out for my aid meant that she thought I could handle anything and everything. This was a more precious gift than any sweater she would ever give me for Christmas. She showed that she had a deep faith in me. I would come to her rescue. I would meet her urgent need. I would take care of her.

That is the very thing that delights the heart of God. When we run to him and throw ourselves upon him in believing prayer, he rejoices. He does not want me out on my own, trying to earn merit stars from him. He wants us, rather, to lean into him, walking with him as closely as possible. He is not so much interested in our *doing* as in our *receiving* from him. After all, what can we do or say or conquer without first receiving grace at God's throne to help us in our time of need? And all that receiving happens through faith.

*Let me depend on God alone:*
*who never changes,*
*who knows what is best for me*
*so much better than I;*
*And gives in a thousand ways, at all times*
*all that the perfect Father can*
*for the son's good growth,*
*things needful, things salutary,*
*things wise, beneficent and happy.*

— ERIC MINER-WHITE

*Christians become strong only by*
*seeing and understanding the grace of God,*
*which is received by faith.*

When troubles rise in your life,
and you don't know what to do,
You'll be fine if you just keep believing.

*O God, early in the morning I cry to you.*
*Help me to pray,*
*and to concentrate my thoughts on you:*
*I cannot do this alone.*

*In me there is darkness,*
*But with you there is light;*
*I am lonely,*
*but you do not leave me;*
*I am feeble in heart,*
*but with you there is help;*
*I am restless*
*but with you there is peace.*
*In me there is bitterness,*
*but with you there is patience;*
*I do not understand your ways,*
*but you know the way for me...*

*Restore me to liberty,*
*And enable me so to live now*
*that I may answer before you and before me.*
*Lord, whatever this day my bring,*
*Your name be praised.*

— DIETRICH BONHOEFFER

I wait for the LORD, my soul waits,

and in his word I put my hope.

My soul waits for the Lord

more than watchmen wait for the morning,

more than watchmen wait for the morning.

— PSALM 130:5-6


I wait for you, O LORD;

you will answer, O Lord my God.

— PSALM 38:15


In the morning, O LORD, you hear my voice;

in the morning I lay my requests before you

and wait in expectation.

— PSALM 5:3


*Prayer is our comfort, strength,*

*and salvation. It's our first line*

*of defense against all of our enemies.*

— MARTIN LUTHER

## PRAYER AND PROMISES

*I am absolutely convinced that the number one*
*reason that Christians today don't pray more*
*is because we do not grasp the connection*
*between prayer and the promises of God.*
*We are trying as individuals and churches*
*to pray "because we're supposed to"*
*without a living faith in the promises of God*
*concerning prayer. No prayer life of any*
*significance can be maintained by this*
*"ought-to" approach. There must be faith*
*in God at the bottom.*

# THE LOST, FOUND

All my talking about prayer faced a severe test several years ago when Carol and I went through the darkest two-and-a-half-year tunnel we could imagine.

Our oldest daughter, Chrissy, had been a model child growing up. But around age sixteen she started to stray. I admit I was slow to notice this—I was too occupied with the church, starting branch congregations, overseeing projects, and all the rest that ministry entails.

Meanwhile, Chrissy not only drew away from us, but also away from God. In time, she even left our home. There were many nights when we had no idea where she was.

As the situation grew more serious, I tried everything. I begged, I pleaded, I scolded, I argued, I tried to control her with money. Looking back, I recognize the foolishness of my actions. Nothing worked; she just hardened more and more. Her boyfriend was everything we did not want for our child.

How I kept functioning through that period I don't know. Many a Sunday morning I would put on my suit, get into the car to drive to the Tabernacle early . . . and cry all the way to the church door. "God, how am I going to get through three meetings today? I'm hanging by a thread." Somehow God would pull my nerves together enough for me to function through another long Sunday.

Like any mother who loves her children, Carol was smitten with tremendous fear and distress. One day she said to me, "Listen, we need to leave New York. I'm serious. This atmosphere has already swallowed up our daughter. We can't keep raising kids here. If you want to stay, you can—but I'm getting our other children out." She wasn't kidding.

Carol wasn't being rebellious; she was just depressed. She elected not to pack up and run after all.

Were we calling on the Lord through all of this? In a sense we were. But I couldn't help jumping in to take action on my own, too. But the more I pressed, the worse Chrissy got.

February came. One cold Tuesday night during the prayer meeting, I talked from Acts 4 about the church boldly calling on God in the face of persecution We entered into a time of prayer, everyone reaching out to the Lord simultaneously.

An usher handed me a note. A young woman whom I felt to be spiritually sensitive had written: *Pastor Cymbala, I feel impressed that we should stop the meeting and all pray for your daughter.*

I hesitated. Was it right to change the flow of the service and focus on my personal need?

Yet something in the note seemed to ring true. I picked up a microphone and told the congregation what had just happened. I said, "Although I haven't talked much about it, my daughter is very far from God these days. She thinks up is down, and down is up; dark is light, and light is dark. But I know God can break through to her, and so I'm going to ask Pastor

Boekstaaf to lead us in praying for Chrissy. Let's all join hands across the sanctuary."

There arose a groaning, a sense of desperate determination, as if to say, "Satan, you will *not* have this girl. Take your hands off her—she's coming back!" I was overwhelmed. The force of that vast throng calling on God almost literally knocked me over.

Thirty-two hours later, on Thursday morning, as I was shaving, Carol suddenly burst through the door, her eyes wide. "Go downstairs!" she blurted. "Chrissy's here."

I headed down the stairs, my heart pounding. As I came around the corner, I saw my daughter on the kitchen *floor*, sobbing. Cautiously I spoke her name: "Chrissy?"

My vision was as clouded by tears as hers. I pulled her up from the floor and held her close as we cried together.

"On Tuesday night, Daddy—who was praying for me? In the middle of the night, God woke me and showed me I was heading toward this abyss. There was no bottom to it—it scared me to death. I was so frightened. I realized how hard I've been, how wrong, how rebellious."

I looked into her bloodshot eyes, and once again I recognized the daughter we had raised.

Chrissy's return to the Lord became evident immediately. Today she is a pastor's wife in the Midwest with three wonderful children.

Lord Jesus, I give you praise:
I was a lost sheep, and you brought me back;
I strayed from your flock, but your shepherd
came and found me.
He sought me out, and brought me
back to be offered
with those sheep prepared for sacrifice.
I was returned to be a child of the apostles,
a brother to those in the west who had
received the crown, and an example to your
people in the east.
Keep them all, do not let them lose the true faith.
Father, Son and Holy Spirit, true God,
Glorious King,
whom all that worship the Holy Trinity, in heaven
and on earth, will ever confess, ages with out end.
Amen.

— GUSTAZAD OF SELEUCIA


God answered [the Israelites'] prayers,
because they trusted in him.

— 1 CHRONICLES 5:20

# NURTURING FAITH

When real faith in God arises, a certainty comes that when we call, he will answer . . . that when we ask, we will receive . . . that when we knock, the door will be opened . . . and soon we find ourselves spending a lot of time in his presence. We seek him for wayward children to be saved, for a greater sense of the Holy Spirit in our church services, for spiritual gifts and power to be released, for the finances we need to do his work.

But I am speaking about more than just presenting a laundry list of requests to God. Faith is especially nurtured when we just wait in God's presence, taking the time to love him and listen for his voice. Strength to keep believing often flows into us as we simply worship the Lord. The promises of Scripture become wonderfully alive as the Spirit applies them to our hearts.

We are always either
drawing nearer to God
or *falling away*.
There is no holding pattern.

Devote yourselves to prayer,
being watchful and thankful.

– COLOSSIANS 4:2

The eyes of the Lord are on the righteous
and his ears are attentive to their prayer.

– 1 PETER 3:12

Humble yourselves, therefore,
under God's mighty hand, that he
may lift you up in due time.
Cast all your anxiety on him because
he cares for you.

– 1 PETER 5:6–7

# THE WORK OF FAITH

*Prayer is the work of faith alone. No one,
except a believer, can truly pray. Believers
don't pray on their own merits, but in the
name of the Son of God, in whom they were
baptized. They're certain that their prayers
please God because he commanded them
to pray in the name of Christ and promised
he would listen to them.*

*Christians pray in response to God's
command and promise. We offer our prayers
to God in the name of Christ, and we know
that what we ask for will be given to us.
We experience God's help in all kinds of needy
situations. And if relief doesn't come soon,
we still know that our prayers are pleasing
to God. We know that God has answered us
because he gives us the strength to endure.*

— MARTIN LUTHER

*Don't give up today because you feel weak
and overwhelmed—that's the very place where
divine power will uphold you if you only
believe and call out to the Lord in total
.dependence. Childlike faith in God is not
only what pleases him but is also the secret
of our strength and power.*

Jesus said, "If you remain in me
and my words remain in you, ask whatever
you wish, and it will be given you."

– J O H N   1 5 : 7

# WALK IN FAITH

Faith enables us to see God on top of all our problems. If we see only the problems, we get depressed and start making wrong decisions. When we have faith, we see God bigger than any mountain, and we know he is going to take care of us.

If *God* is for you, it doesn't matter how many demons in hell try to oppose you. If *God* is for you, it doesn't matter what your opponents whisper in the ears of people. Unbelief has a devious way of envisioning negative things. When you're walking in faith, you get out of bed in the morning saying, "Surely goodness and love will follow me all the days of my life, and I will dwell in the house of the LORD forever" (Psalm 23:6). But when you're walking in unbelief, you get out of bed saying, "Oh, no! Is this the day I'm going to lose it all?" The glass is always half-empty.

Those who walk in faith are still realists. They often admit that they don't know how everything is going to work out; but they insist that their God will supply nonetheless.

Unbelief loves to paint the bleakest picture it can. It loves to get us mumbling to ourselves, I'm not going to make it. I just know this is going to turn out terrible. The future is bound to crash on me.

*Let me tell you that God, who began a good work in you, is not about to stop now. After sending his Son to die for your sins, after saving you at such incredible cost, why would he let you fail now?*

*Let us declare war this very moment on the cleverness that is really a mask for unbelief. Bring your problem to God, as a little child would, in total confidence that he alone can fix whatever is broken. Open your Bible and let the Holy Spirit plant in you the seeds of a fresh faith that will blossom as you wait on the Lord. Don't give up asking, seeking, and knocking—no matter what pressure you feel to "do something."*

*If you but trust in God to guide you*

*and place your confidence in him,*

*You'll find him always there beside you*

*to give you hope and strength within;*

*For those who trust God's changeless love*

*build on a rock that will not move.*

— GEORG NEWMARK

If...you seek the Lord your God,
you will find him if you look for him
with all your heart and with all your soul.

— DEUTERONOMY 4:29

I am the LORD, your God,
who takes hold of your right hand
and says to you, Do not fear;
I will help you.

— ISAIAH 41:13

Cast your cares on the LORD
and he will sustain you;
he will never let the righteous fall.

— PSALM 55:22

# BEYOND BELIEVING

*Sending leads to preaching.*
*Preaching leads to hearing.*
*Hearing leads to believing.*
*Believing leads to calling on the name of the Lord.*

*Notice that believing is not the climax.*
*Even the great Protestant Reformers who taught*
*us the principle of sola fide ("faith alone")*
*also preached that intellectual assent alone*
*does not bring salvation. There is one more step*
*for demonstrating a real and living faith,*
*and that is calling out to God with all*
*of one's heart and soul.*

Possibly there is a need in your life today to stop all the struggling with your own strength. Let it go, and call out to God in simple faith. Remember that no one has ever been disappointed after putting trust in him. Not one person throughout all of human history has ever depended upon God and found that God let him down. Never! Not once!

Face the obvious fact that the problem or need is far too big for you to handle. Use the very fact of your inadequacy as a springboard to a new, wholehearted trust in God's unfailing promises.

"If my people, who are called by my name, will humble themselves and pray and seek my face and turn from their wicked ways, then will I hear from heaven and will forgive their sin and will heal their land," says the Lord.

– 2 Chronicles 7:14

*Going into a private room and locking the door isn't required when you pray. However, you might want to be alone to pour out your wants and needs to God with words and gestures that you wouldn't feel comfortable having others see. Although you can pray in your heart without saying anything aloud, words and gestures help kindle the spirit.*

*So the Christian's entire life should be devoted to God—spreading his Word and praising his kingdom. Whatever a Christian does must be grounded in sincere prayer.*

– Martin Luther

The Power of Prayers of Faith 129

# GOD ANSWERS OUR CALL

At that time men began to call
on the name of the LORD.

— GENESIS 4:26

Think about that. Until then, people had known God mainly as the Creator. He had made the Garden of Eden and the rest of the world as far as their eyes could see.

Now came the beginning of the first collective relationship with the Almighty. Before a Bible was available, before the first preacher was ordained or the first choir formed, a godly string of men and women distinguished themselves from their ungodly neighbors by calling on the Lord. Cain and his posterity had gone their own way, independent of God. By contrast, these people affirmed their dependence on God by calling out to him.

In fact, God's first people were not called "Jews" or "the children of Israel" or "Hebrews." In the very beginning their original name was "those who call on the name of the LORD."

On some unmarked day . . . at some unnoted hour. . . a God-placed instinct in human hearts came alive. People sensed that if you are in trouble and you call out to God, he will answer you! He will intervene in your situation.

I can imagine one woman saying to another, "Have you heard about the God who answers when you call on him? He's more than just the Creator; he cares and responds to our needs. He actually understands what we're feeling."

"What are you talking about? God does whatever he pleases; people can't influence him one way or the other."

"No, no you're wrong. When you call out to him he doesn't turn a deaf ear. He listens! He responds. He acts."

# PRAYER CHANGES US

You might wonder, "why does God insist that we pray to him and tell him our problems? Why doesn't he take care of us without our having to ask? He already knows what we need better than we do." God continually showers his gifts on the whole world every day. He gives people sunshine, rain, good harvests, money, healthy bodies, and so on. But no one asks God for these gifts or thanks him for them. If God already knows that we can't live without lights or food for any length of time, then why does he want us to ask for these necessities?

Obviously, he doesn't command us to pray in order to inform him about our needs. God gives us his gifts freely and abundantly. He wants us to recognize that he is willing and able to give us even more. When we pray, we're not telling God anything he doesn't already know. Rather, we are the ones gaining knowledge and insight. Asking God to supply our needs keeps us from becoming like the unbelieving skeptics, who don't acknowledge God and don't thank him for his many gifts.

All of this teaches us to acknowledge God's generosity even more. Because we continue to search for him and keep on knocking at his door, he showers us with more and more blessings. Everything we have is a gift from God. When we pray, we should express our gratitude by saying,

"Lord, I know that I can't create a single slice of my daily bread. You are the only one who can supply all of my needs. I have no way to protect myself from disasters. You know what I need ahead of time, so I'm convinced that you will take care of me."

– MARTIN LUTHER

# TALKING TO OURSELVES

Unbelief talks to itself instead of talking to God. When we talk to ourselves, we're not talking to anyone very smart, because our outlook is very limited. But if we talk to God, we're talking to someone who knows everything. He knows what he promised in the beginning, and he knows exactly how to fulfill those promises no matter the circumstances.

Trust in the LORD with all your heart
and lean not on your own understanding.

— PROVERBS 3:5

I love the LORD, for he heard my voice;
he heard my cry for mercy.
Because he turned his ear to me,
I will call on him as long as I live.

— PSALM 116:1-2

# GOD'S
# ACCOMPLISHMENTS

Every attempt to do something significant for God is never simple. Whenever God stirs us to establish his kingdom in a new place, the enemy is sure to taunt us. The devil always tries to convince us that we've tackled too much this time and we'll soon be humiliated.

If we are courageous enough to go on the spiritual attack, to be mighty men and women of prayer and faith, there is no limit to what God can accomplish through us. Some of us will turn out to be famous; the rest will remain obscure. That doesn't matter. What counts is bringing God's power and light into a dark world.

No personal or church situation is too hopeless for the all-sufficient power of the Holy Spirit. God will be no more eager to act tomorrow than he is right now. He is waiting for us to take his promises seriously and go boldly to the throne of grace. He wants us to meet the enemy at the very point of attack, standing against him in the name of Christ. When we do so, God will back us up with all the resources of heaven.

Pray in the Spirit on all occasions

with all kinds of prayers and requests.

— EPHESIANS 6:18

# THE POWER
## OF PRAYERS
## OF FAITH

# PRAYER BORN
# OF THE SPIRIT

We Christians seldom admit that we don't know how to pray. Many of us have been taught since childhood how to put sentences together that sound like a prayer, to the point that we are professionals at it. Some can turn out an eloquent presentation to God at a moment's notice.

Prayer born of the Spirit, however, is another dimension of calling on God to the point of having the Holy Spirit supernaturally assist us. This is not a worked-up emotionalism but a powerful promise of help from God himself!

The Spirit helps us in our weakness.
We do not know what we ought to pray for,
but the Spirit himself intercedes for us with
groans that words cannot express.

— ROMANS 8:26


But you, dear friends, build yourselves
up in your most holy faith and pray in the
Holy Spirit.

— JUDE 20


May the God of hope fill you with all joy
and peace as you trust in him, so that
you may overflow with hope by the power
of the Holy Spirit.

— ROMANS 15:13

*I have learned from my own experience that
praying is often the most difficult thing to do.
I don't hold myself up as a master of prayer.
In fact, I admit that I have often said these
words coldly: "God, have mercy on me."
I prayed that way because I was worried
about my own unworthiness.
Yet, ultimately, the Holy Spirit convinced me,
"No matter how you feel, you must pray!"
God wants you to pray, and he wants
to hear your prayers—not because you are
worthy, but because he is merciful.*

— MARTIN LUTHER

*O Holy Spirit,*
*Giver of light and life,*
*impart to us thoughts higher than*
*our own thoughts,*
*and prayers better than our own prayers,*
*and powers beyond our own powers,*
*that we may spend and be spent*
*in the ways of love and goodness,*
*after the perfect image*
*of our Lord and Savior Jesus Christ.*

— ERIC MILNER-WHITE
AND G.W. BRIGGS

# INTO GOD'S WILL

In the fall of 1994 I was invited to speak at a Christian music gathering in Indianapolis. I arrived on a Thursday, and that evening I still wasn't sure what I should speak about the next morning. I was leaning toward a simple message of encouragement— one I had preached before. I thought it would go well in this festive setting. I certainly didn't want to do anything controversial or get in anybody's face about anything.

I went to part of the evening concert but left around eight o-clock to return to my hotel room. There I began to seek the Lord about my message for the next morning. I reviewed my sermon outline and then went to prayer. The longer I prayed, the more this nice, familiar sermon idea went dead inside of me.

In time I felt drawn toward the text "My house will be called a house of prayer" (Mark 11:17), a message I had preached not long before at the Brooklyn Tabernacle. It's a very direct message. It deals with Jesus' cleaning the merchants out of the temple and pointedly calls the audience to what the church is really for, as opposed to all the misuses we make of it.

I began to argue with the Lord. A sermon on cleaning merchants out of the house of God—at a music festival? Surely not! But it was getting late. I had no notes for that message anyway. I could remember only parts and pieces of what I had preached at home. Surely I wasn't going to get up in front of 10,000 people and just "wing it."

Yet the Holy Spirit seemed to persistently whisper to my heart, *This is why I brought you here. This is what I want you to preach. Are you going to do my will, or are you just going to go out there tomorrow morning and "perform"?*

I kept struggling in prayer. Finally, after an hour or two, I relented. I opened my Bible to the passage in Mark as I said, "God, help me. If you want to use this to speak to the people tomorrow morning, all right. Show me how to reconstruct this sermon."

Around midnight something very unusual happened. I was attacked by a tremendous feeling of fear and insecurity. I began to imagine the audience turning against me. Something or someone kept whispering to me that this "prophetic" message wasn't going to fit the setting at all. It seemed as if I was battling against forces intent on disrupting this message I now felt so strongly.

The sun had just come up that Friday morning. On less than four hours' sleep, I began getting read for the day ahead. All too soon I was across the street at the arena. As the host began to introduce me, I walked out onto the stage and nervously took stock of what I was up against. *O God, help me now!* I prayed silently.

I began speaking in a soft voice. "I want to talk for a few moments about something so vital, and yet it's so simple. It's so familiar to us—and that's the danger. I want our session this morning to be something that will make a difference in our lives. . . . "

It seemed that the longer I spoke, the more clarity came into my heart. I felt calm inside. I could sense the Holy Spirit helping me. I was just pouring out what I felt God wanted me to say. Some of the last sentences I uttered were, "God says that when you call, he will answer. The hard cases some of you are facing today—the answer won't come from another seminar. . . . We have too many mere technicians who are only stressing methodology, and they are increasingly invading the church. The answer is not in any human methodology. The answer is in the power of the Holy Spirit. The answer is in the grace of God."

I walked off the stage. Inside I felt peace: God had indeed helped me do what he wanted in that place.

What happened to me in Indianapolis was not unusual. It was merely the Holy Spirit coming to the aid of a human vessel who didn't really know what he was supposed to be doing. The Spirit is the one who leads us into God's will.

# GOD'S EQUATION

God has given us a very simple equation if only we have the faith to reach out and experience it:

The Holy Spirit's power is our greatest need.

This power and blessing is freely promised to all God's people.

This promise can only be fully received through sincere praying in faith and through waiting on God for his blessing to come.

This is what happened in the New Testament, and this is the only thing that will satisfy our souls' thirst. A decade of gadget and gimmicks will never accomplish what God the Holy Spirit can do in one month as he works in the life of a church.

*Lord, Lord, Lord, please come to help me;*
*I turn to you alone for my refuge.*

— AGATHONICE OF PERGAMOS

Repent and be baptized, every one of you,
in the name of Jesus Christ for the forgiveness
of your sins. And you will receive the gift
of the Holy Spirit. The promise is for you
and your children and for all who are far off—
for all whom the Lord our God will call.

– ACTS 2:38-39


Those who live in accordance with the Spirit
have their minds set on what the Spirit desires.

– ROMANS 8:5


Those who are led by the Spirit of God
are sons of God.

– ROMANS 8:14

*O God, the Holy Spirit,*
*come to us, and among us:*
*come as the wind, and cleanse us;*
*come as the fire, and burn;*
*come as the dew, and refresh:*
*convict, convert, and consecrate*
*many hearts and lives*
*to our great good*
*and they greater glory,*
*and this we ask for Jesus Christ's sake.*

— ERIC MILNER-WHITE

The Holy Spirit is still greater than all our shortcomings and failures. He has come to free us from the restraints and complexes of insufficient talents, intelligence, or upbringing. He intends to do through us what only he can do.

The Holy Spirit is the Spirit of prayer. Only when we are full of the Spirit do we feel the need for God everywhere we turn. We can be driving a car, and spontaneously our spirit starts going up to God with needs and petitions and intercessions right there in the middle of traffic.

# THE POWER OF THE SPIRIT

Standing six-feet-four, Willie McLean is our church's head of security and walks with me every Sunday as I move in and out of our four crowded services. What an irony that he should be serving God in this line of work, since his "rap sheet" with the NYPD is, as the saying goes, as long as your arm. If you read it, you would say Willis was absolutely hopeless, truly incorrigible—just lock him up and throw away the key.

Willie started off horribly in junior high by getting his girlfriend pregnant—the twelve-year-old daughter of a New York City cop. "I didn't know she was only twelve," he says with a shy smile. When Elise gave birth to the baby, her parents tried to keep things quiet...until the next year, when the young couple did it again!

By his junior year of high school, Willie had dropped out, preferring to spend his days in the pool rooms of Harlem or out with the street hustlers. He also began stealing cars. At age seventeen Willie started experimenting with drugs.

"It seemed like I could not stop going to jail," Willie remembers. "I kept getting ninety days for this, sixty days for that: writing 'numbers'. . . trespassing...disorderly conduct...shoplifting from Macy's. It seemed like the streets just kept calling my name. . . . " Eventually, twenty-one counts of armed robbery led to a ten-year sentence.

When Willie finally got out of prison in 1976, Elise and the two children were amazingly still waiting for him. The couple got married at last, over the strong protest of her family. But the angry twenty-seven-year-old Willie was still out of control.

After the death of a daughter from diabetes, Willie became all the more violent. He stole $20,000 in drugs from a supplier, sold them, and used the money to enter the prostitution business. Soon, however, the cash flow could not keep up with his expenses. Before long, the drug supplier figured out who the culprit was and put out a contract on Willie's life.

Willie was making a call at a public phone booth one day when, all of a sudden, bullets started flying. Willie twisted in first one direction and then the other as a 9mm bullet bounced off the phone and into his face. Passing through his tongue, the bullet split his jaw. Meanwhile, another bullet entered his shoulder from the back.

Lying on the street, watching his blood run toward the gutter, Willie prayed for one of the few times in his life: "God, please don't let me go out like this."

When Elise, who had recently started attending

our church, came to visit him in the hospital this time, she just stared. She showed no emotion at all.

"Aren't you going to cry?" Willie asked.

"No, I'm gonna pray for you. You need Jesus bad...."

But Willie McLean was not yet ready to change. He met another girlfriend named Brigitte, who bore him two more children in the coming years. Brigitte's incensed mother tried to have him killed as well, but Willie managed to charm the designated gunmen into leaving him alone.

He did not fare so well with the police in Jamaica, Queens, however, after they photographed him from a rooftop making a drug sale. The sentence this time was a year on Rikers Island plus five years' probation. And that was the point when Elise finally managed to get her thirty-nine-year-old husband to our church.

"The choir began singing that day," he recalls, "and I just opened up. My nose started running, and then I was actually crying!"

Before Willie knew it, an invitation to come to Christ began. At the front of the church he spread out his arms and cried, "O God—I just can't take it anymore. I can't go on. . . . "

Today Willie explains in his soft-spoken voice, "The Lord didn't just save me—he delivered me. He mended my marriage. He gave back my self-esteem. God has turned my life inside out. He has blessed me and my family incredibly."

The power of the Holy Spirit got a hold of this giant of a man and stopped his self-destruction. And the same Spirit of God who turned Willie McLean to Christ and salvation has kept him clean and victorious ever since. Think of the power potential we have available to us through God's Word anointed by the Holy Spirit. Not just the Word only, nor an emphasis solely on the Spirit—we must have the Word and the Spirit together bringing blessing and salvation.

Jesus said, "You will receive power
when the Holy Spirit comes on you."

— ACTS 1:8

The mind of sinful man is death, but the
mind controlled by the Spirit is life and peace.

— ROMANS 8:6

Because you are sons, God sent the
Spirit of his Son into our hearts,
the Spirit who calls out, "Abba, Father."

— GALATIANS 4:6

# TOTAL ATTENTION

Paul could have said: "God has sent the Spirit of his Son into us to pray: 'Abba, Father.'" But he purposely says "calls out" to indicate the anguish of the Christian who is still weak and needs to grow in the faith.

But in the middle of trials and conflicts, it's difficult to call out to God, and it takes a lot of effort to cling to God's Word. At those times, we cannot perceive Christ. We do not see him. Our heart doesn't feel his presence and his help during the attack. All this raises very powerful and horrible shouts against us so that there does not appear to be anything left but despair and eternal death.

However, in the middle of these terrors of the law, the thundering of sin, the shaking of death, and the roar of the devil, the Holy Spirit in our hearts begins to call out, "Abba! Father!" And his cry is much stronger and drowns out the powerful and horrible shouts of the law, sin, death, and the devil. It penetrates through the clouds and heaven and reaches up to the ears of God.

— MARTIN LUTHER

*Almighty God, Father of our*
*Lord Jesus Christ, grant, we pray,*
*that we might be grounded and settled*
*in your truth by the coming*
*of your Holy Spirit into our hearts.*
*What we do not know,*
*reveal to us;*
*What is lacking within us,*
*make complete;*
*That which we do know,*
*confirm in us;*
*And keep us blameless in your service,*
*through Jesus Christ our Lord.*

— CLEMENT OF ROME

# FRESH POWER

God will act whenever and wherever his people slow down long enough to give him their total attention in faith-filled prayer, praise, and worshipful waiting. He will transform our lives, invade and bless our churches, and equip us to do things beyond "all we [could] ask or imagine, according to his power that is *at work within us*" (Ephesians 3:20). May fresh power begin this very day to work in and through us as we yield ourselves totally to the Spirit of the living God.

*Please, God, send
the Holy Spirit
upon us and revive
your people.*

Also Available from
Inspirio and Jim Cymbala

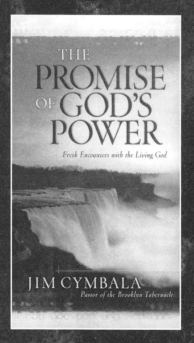

THE
PROMISE
OF GOD'S
POWER

*Fresh Encounters with the Living God*

JIM CYMBALA
*Pastor of the Brooklyn Tabernacle*

# SOURCES

Appleton, George. *The Oxford Book of Common Prayer.* Copyright 1985 by George Appleton. New York, NY: Oxford University Press,1988.

Arnold, Duane W. H. *Prayers of the Martyrs.* Copyright 1991 by Duane W. H. Arnold. Grand Rapids, MI: Zondervan Publishing House, 1991.

Cymbala, Jim with Dean Merrill. *Fresh Faith.* Copyright 1999 by Jim Cymbala. Grand Rapids, MI: ZondervanPublishingHouse, 1999.

Cymbala, Jim with Dean Merrill. *Fresh Power.* Copyright 2001 by Jim Cymbala. Grand Rapids, MI: ZondervanPublishingHouse, 2001.

Cymbala, Jim with Dean Merrill. *Fresh Wind, Fresh Fire.* Copyright 1997 by Jim Cymbala. Grand Rapids, MI: Zondervan Publishing House, 1997.

Luther, Martin. *By Faith Alone.* Copyright 1998 by Jim Galvin. Grand Rapids, MI: World Publishing, 1998.

At Inspirio we love to hear from you—your
stories, your feedback,
and your product ideas.
Please send your comments to us
by way of e-mail at
icares@zondervan.com
or to the address below:

inspirio™

Attn: Inspirio Cares
5300 Patterson Avenue SE
Grand Rapids, MI 49530

If you would like further information
about Inspirio and the products we
create please visit us at:
www.inspiriogifts.com

Thank you and God Bless!